# ······· HOW TO GO ·······
# BEYOND
# STRENGTH

*Learn Transformative Strategies For Personal Growth,
Elevate Your Potential, Master Resilience, and Create
Incredible Life-Changing Success*

by

## J P PATHAK

**Email:** jppathak1@gmail.com

## DEDICATION

To my loving daughters, **Juhi** and **Garima**.

In the tapestry of life, your unwavering support, and boundless encouragement have been the vibrant threads that have woven the fabric of this book. Your wisdom, kindness, and belief in my journey fuelled my determination, and your willingness to stand by me through every chapter of this endeavour has made the climb worthwhile. You have been instrumental in shaping these pages, contributing to the narrative in ways- both seen and unseen. This work is as much yours as it is mine.

Thank you for being the pillars of support that held me steady during the storms of creation.

With Love and Gratitude.

*J P Pathak*

## ACKNOWLEDGMENT

To my mentor and cherished colleagues whose collaborative spirit has infused joy and inspiration into every step of this writing experience. This book stands as a testament to our shared journey. Your collective wisdom, friendship, and shared experiences have enriched my life beyond measure. They have made my life journey a memorable one.

My sincere thanks to Mr. GV Prasad Co-Chairman @ Dr.Reddy's Laboratories for inspiring me and encouraging me to write this book.

J P Pathak

## WHY IS THIS BOOK FOR YOU?

*By writing this book, I want you to believe that your future is much brighter than your past.*

*In my first book, "The One Thing," we explored the key element that leads to success. I got a very positive response from many of you, and it has encouraged me to write this book. Today, I am so excited to introduce my latest creation to you. 'A Journey from Strength to Strength' S*

*Building upon the foundation laid in the first book, our exploration of strengths continues. The lesson within these pages will not only help you enhance your strengths but also empower you to uncover and cultivate new ones. The central character, Ramdas, introduced in the 1st episode, will continue to be our guide. I am so happy to share with you that Ramdas was liked by many of you.*

*So, let us embark on this journey together, where strength meets resilience, and success is not just a destination but a continuous evolution.*

*This book is designed in two sections, in section one you will find the role of a leader in team building, the key elements of team building, and the importance of team building, and in section two you will find all about self-reflection. What and why of Self–Reflection in detail.*

**Benjamin Franklin said- "An investment in knowledge pays the best interest."**

Discover the journey of 'Strength to Strength'- a guide to personal growth and enhanced success. Investing in this book ensures a meaningful exploration of your potential. Cultivate your strength and pave the way for a more successful and fulfilling life.

## FOREWORD

During the initial years of my managerial career, I was very keen on developing my team.

My focus used to be on the 'Areas of Improvement.'

But somehow, instead of seeing the desired improvement, I found that such interactions around 'Areas of Improvement' invariably brought tension and resistance, making my reportees feel demotivated and leaving me frustrated.

After many years of frustration, I finally realized that the whole approach of trying to improve the person by focusing on his weakness is flawed.

Then I discovered one of the biggest lessons of my life:

"Focusing on our and other's *strengths* creates a transformative effect and opens the door to exponential results."

So, when I saw the title of this book that talks about going **beyond strengths,** I knew I had to read it.

Since I had loved reading J P Pathak's earlier book, "The 1 Thing," I read this book with high expectations.

And this book exceeded my expectations!!

If you are a mid-level manager aiming to make it to the top or someone who has just begun your career, either way, this book is for you.

This is not just a one-time read. This book is for keeps.

This book will serve you as a constant companion as you climb up your career ladder.

In today's world, there is no dearth of information. But what is rare is wise advice learned through years of experience.

That's precisely what you get by reading **HOW TO GO BEYOND STRENGTH.**

In addition to a long and successful career in sales and marketing, J P Pathak also handled the L&D function. He has trained thousands of sales personnel and line managers to go beyond their strengths.

Hence, it is a matter of great pleasure and honour for me to write the foreword for this book.

Wishing you a great success in your career.

*Miliind Harrdas*
*Author of Internation bestseller on Creativity:*
*Ideas on Demand: A Crash Course on Creativity*

In a world where strength is often equated with success, it's easy to overlook the power of going beyond mere physical or tangible abilities. In "How To Go Beyond Strength," the author J. P. Pathak delves deep into the realms of leadership, team building, and self-reflection, offering a profound exploration of what it truly means to excel in both professional and personal spheres.

Organized into two insightful sections, this book serves as a guiding light for individuals seeking to harness the full potential of their leadership capabilities and personal growth journey.

The first section meticulously examines the pivotal role of a leader in the art of team building. Drawing from years of experience and research, the author elucidates the key elements that underpin effective team dynamics. From fostering trust and communication to cultivating a shared vision, each chapter is a blueprint for leaders aspiring to create high-performing teams. Through compelling anecdotes and practical strategies, readers are invited to rethink their approach to leadership, understanding that true strength lies not in domination, but in collaboration and empowerment.

I was fascinated by the SOAR Technique.

**SOAR** above the rest and chart your development path!

Forget the dusty SWOT analysis, SOAR offers a dynamic approach to personal and professional development.

This four-step method empowers you to take flight, leveraging your strengths (S) and identifying promising opportunities (O) to craft ambitious aspirations (A). The journey culminates in achieving tangible results (R), ensuring your goals take off and land successfully.

Imagine pinpointing your unique skills and experiences as strengths. Perhaps you're a creative problem solver or a master communicator.

Next, scan the horizon for opportunities, like emerging trends or skills in demand. Maybe you envision learning data analysis or mastering public speaking.

Now, let your aspirations soar! Combine your strengths with these opportunities to set audacious goals. Perhaps you aim to lead a data-driven marketing campaign or launch a captivating podcast.

Finally, focus on results. What metrics will demonstrate your success? Quantifiable achievements keep you grounded and ensure your aspirations translate into reality.

SOAR isn't just a one-time exercise. Regularly revisit your strengths, explore new opportunities, and refine your aspirations. With each iteration, you'll discover new heights to reach, ensuring your development journey is as inspiring as the results you achieve.

Transitioning seamlessly into the second section, the focus shifts inward towards the profound practice of self-reflection. In a world characterized by constant noise and distraction, the ability to pause and introspect is a rare gift. Here, the author invites readers on a transformative journey of self-discovery, prompting them to delve deep into their thoughts, emotions, and aspirations. By unraveling the what and why of self-reflection, readers are equipped with the tools to navigate life's complexities with clarity and purpose. Through meditation exercises, and reflective practices, individuals are empowered to cultivate a deeper understanding of themselves and their place in the world.

As I journeyed through the pages of "How To Go Beyond Strength," I was struck by the J. P. Pathak's unwavering commitment to authenticity and growth. This book is not merely a guide, but a manifesto for those who dare to challenge the status quo and embrace the transformative power of vulnerability and self-awareness. Whether you're a seasoned leader or an aspiring visionary, the wisdom contained within these pages will undoubtedly inspire you to transcend limitations and strive for greatness in every aspect of your life.

Prepare to embark on a journey of discovery, empowerment, and limitless possibility. Your path to going beyond strength starts here.

*Vivek Hattangadi*
*Chief Mentor at 'B - Black Belt Brand Builders'*
*(earlier 'The Enablers)*

How to Go- Beyond Strength is about 12 dimensions of Leadership approaches and traits essential for any leader in various phases of their leadership journey.

JP has mastered the art of articulating complex use cases ( multiple in this book ) and situations to be narrated in a story mode making it Lucid and interesting for the reader to remain engaged as they move from one topic to another.

All topics are equally relevant but currently being part of a transformation role –"Being Empathetic " and " Embrace the change " resonated most with me.

I read it somewhere that when a leader starts his career he gets hired for his IQ but as time passes and he goes through his journey of being a team leader, many a times he gets fired for his EQ.

JP's book is a smart guide for young leaders to learn the softer aspects of Leadership to be successful in their careers.

*Ashish Nigam*
*Head – Transformation (FF)*
*@Dr, Reddy's Laboratories Ltd*

# TABLE OF CONTENTS

# TRUE LEADER IN ACTION

## STRENGTH-TO-STRENGTH - MY EXAMPLE

In December 2007, during a brainstorming session for budget planning for the fiscal year 2008-09, I met with my colleagues in Gurugram to discuss the meaning of "strength to strength" and its significance for us. The weather was cold, and we were in the middle of an interesting discussion: what shall we do to make the division stronger than yesterday? What is our strength, and what has made our division so successful? This was the moment when one of our colleagues brought a new dimension to the table- we must add strength to our current strength. All of us were happy to listen to the word, add strength to strength. Our leader accepted that word and asked us to list our current strengths; only then can we add strength to our current strengths. We are good at what? We accepted the idea and did many exercises to conclude current strengths. One very interesting thing happened during that meeting: we are doing well, our team is successful, people are earning good incentives, and they are happy. Our leader challenged this statement, and he asked us- "Is good enough?" this made us realize that we need to strive for the next level of performance to be truly successful. Thanks to my leader for asking a really thought-provoking question.

Another interesting thing happened during that meeting; we discussed what we would not do. This is called a trade-off; my experience suggests to me that many leaders fail here. Everyone wants to do better and wants to do everything possible to be successful; only some are there who know- what they will not do and also will not allow others to do.

We had our list of what to do and what not to do ready; we all were satisfied with our contribution to the meeting. We worked very hard and made history by making the biggest team with the highest growth within the organization.

I would suggest you to prepare your list of:

- To do

- Not to do

- Do more and

- Do less

It's important to note that everyone perceives success differently, and nobody joins a job to fail. However, some people may have low self-esteem and lack confidence, preventing them from behaving like true professionals. I am grateful to my leaders for asking such a thought-provoking question and helping me understand the difference between being successful and more successful. The following incident was shared by one of my very close friends; this event changed my perception of the profession. I will remain grateful to my friend; unfortunately, he is not among us now.

It was October of 2002, and after many successful quarters and years, this was a very low month for me in terms of performance. I rate that performance below par and at an acceptable level. The most unfortunate part was that I could not anticipate this. I had a terrible mood and was disturbed because of my poor performance. The Zone will not be able to perform satisfactorily. I was expecting a call from my coach and my mentor, and honestly speaking, I did not have an answer for such a debacle. I was continuously thinking of the answer ( I can say excuses and not real answers as I did not have any). I am still waiting to receive a call from him. I could not sleep the whole night because of such bad shape, and I was thinking of quitting the profession.

The next day, I dialled his landline number at his home, and his wife answered the phone. I got a message that I would get a call from his office around 10 AM, so I should wait. It was around 8.00 AM, and I had roughly 2 Hours to decide and think about my future; in the meantime, I wrote my resignation letter.

I was feeling relieved but was not sure about what I should do next.

I got a call at 10 AM Sharp, and we shared pleasantry. Then there was a big pause, and I was emotionally weak as well; my boss took the initiative and said, will it be OK if we connect at 4 PM? By the time you can complete your review with yourself and find out possible reasons, what is the plan for November month? I could say nothing, and I asked for permission and said Sir, I want to quit. There was no response for a few seconds, and then there was a simple question: You did it deliberately? Can you do anything for this performance, even if you try your best? I did not have any answer for this too,

He said after a pause, forget this as a bad dream and do proper analysis and discuss what went wrong and what you will do differently next time. And that will be more important for me than the Oct performance.

Can You imagine such a great leader? Do you wish to have a leader like him? Or Do you want to be a leader like him?

I am sure you have developed a huge respect for him, and surely you want to be a leader like him.

That is good news, and I am sure this book will help you be a great leader tomorrow.

**STORY #1**

In 2005, a Reputed Pharmaceutical company needed to do better, and its major brands were de-growing. The company's senior leadership was not able to fix the cause, so they were not able to make a decision for those brands and how to take the company on a growth path. Some ideas were shared, and the company agreed to launch a new division with those de-growing brands. Now, the challenge was about who would take responsibility for managing the business. When brands are de-growing, the morale of the team is low, and it becomes more difficult to manage the team; the possibility of attrition is very high. Existing leaders were not willing to take risks. Against the advice of many, one of the young leaders came forward to accept the challenge. This leader, filled with positivity and the collective spirit of a team, took over the charge and picked up his core team in sales and marketing. At the time of crisis, instead of focusing on targets and timelines, he invested time in understanding his team members. Their strengths and fostering a culture of collaboration and encouragement.

One day, he called a meeting in the conference room, and we all were there in the meeting room with anticipation filled in the air. He welcomed us with a genuine smile on his face. He started with his vision of the division and company. It was not just about financial success; it was about creating a culture where everyone felt valued and inspired to give his best. We all started believing the leadership style of our leader, and very soon, the environment of optimism was everywhere in the team. The once stressful environment transformed into a nurturing environment where creativity flourished and performance soared. We organized many team-building events. Over some time, this team was the best-performing team. One of my colleagues said in a team meeting- "I never thought a workplace could feel like a second home." This is the true power of positive leadership. Blissful innovation continued till the team won the highest award in the company- "The Chairman's Excellence Award." Great Leader, Great Leadership, and a Wonderful Team!

We should also be clear about what will not help individuals. It is equally important to know. Why is it so important? We can learn from this situation.

### STORY #2

There was a mechanic who used to fix faults on telephones when we had a black handset at our home. One day, this mechanic came to repair a phone at the residence of a gentleman. When the doorbell rang, he was welcomed by the lady of the house and shown the phone set. He started to examine the set with all seriousness, and the process took more than 30 minutes. The lady of the house was very caring, so she offered him a cup of tea with some snacks. This process continued for more than two hours, and the lady, with a lot of anger in her mind, said with a polite tone of voice, "Gentleman, you should repair the helicopter. You will get more money there." The engineer, in a delighted mood, said, "Thank you, Madam, for your suggestions, but I do not know how to repair the helicopter." The lady, with a sarcastic smile on her face, said, "Anyway, you do not know how to repair the phone either, but still, you are trying your level best.".

This kind of approach will not help you to add any strength to your current strength.

What is the most important thing?

Identifying your core strength is the most important thing.

But How? Let us discuss this in detail.

# LEARNING SOAR

**SOAR is a technique to identify strength and aspiration.**

The question is how he can add strength to his current strength. He may have skills to deliver, but did he know?

So, as a young leader, you must check for their understanding. Please provide them with the required knowledge and encourage them to learn more about the subject. Help them sharpen their skills to do better and deliver results on time.

It is important not only to put in great effort but also to direct them effectively with the right knowledge in order to achieve the desired results.

Some individuals need to recognize their strengths and seek validation from others, but this approach may only sometimes be helpful. There are only a few individuals who truly care about your growth and are willing to support you. In my book "The One Thing," I have delved into this concept of trust and belief with examples. I highly recommend that you read it to gain a better understanding of this important topic. To be more confident and successful, you have to go from strength to strength.

I am sharing a few important aspects of strength to build on.

Start with SOAR analysis; you can do this analysis for your brands and your team as well. It was invented by Jacqueline Stavros, David Cooperrider & D. Lynn Kelley in the year 2003

SOAR is an approach to strategic planning. This tool helps you analyze your current strengths and opportunities, and you can create a vision for the future.

**S- Strength**

**O- Opportunity**

**A- Aspiration and**

**R- Results**

The SOAR technique involves using appreciative inquiry, which involves making people feel comfortable. An example of this technique is when I noticed one of my first-line managers wearing a very expensive watch. As it was unlikely that he could afford such a watch, I didn't want to offend him by asking directly. Instead, I used an appreciative inquiry approach and said to him, "Your watch looks very elegant; it must have been costly, too." He smiled and replied, "You're right; it was very costly here in India. My brother-in-law, who works as a VP in this company, gifted it to me on my birthday." This technique allowed me to get the answer to my question without hurting his self-esteem.

**STRENGTH**

Identify the strength of your team and the strength of your Organization- where is your organization doing well? **So you**

**can build on that strength. In the same way,** you can identify the strengths of your team members.

## OPPORTUNITY

How can you delight your customers? Customer satisfaction and customer delight are the same. When you meet the expectations of your customers, it is called customer satisfaction, and when you exceed the expectations, it is called customer delight.

There was a small-budget hotel at Meerut where both my coach and I used to stay. One day, my coach arrived at the hotel very late and was feeling very hungry. He asked the hotel manager if he could get something to eat, but he was worried that the kitchen might be closed since it was midnight. He was only expecting to get something simple like bread, butter, or a sandwich with tea. However, to his surprise, the hotel manager asked him what he would like to eat and offered to prepare his choice of food in just 20 minutes. While he waited, the manager also offered him a cup of coffee. When the hot meal of his choice was ready, he was delighted. This is an example of customer delight, where satisfied customers become repeat customers.

### ASPIRATION

What do you want to achieve in life? What do you want to achieve in your professional life in the next few years?

As explained by Stephen R Covey in his book, "7 Habits of Highly Effective People,"- Begin with the end in mind.

It's important to have a clear vision or goal in mind when considering the kind of results you want to achieve. For instance, do you want to become a leader in middle or senior management? Or could you aim to make your team the number one performer in various aspects? You may want to start your own business. There are many examples of people who started with the end goal in mind, such as...

"Steve Jobs had a crystal clear vision for his brainchild, his product Apple - how it will be an exceptional product.

John F. Kennedy, the former President of America, was clear about the historical achievement of successfully landing a man on the Moon by the end of 1960.

Bill Gates was clear about how his product Microsoft would function and would revolutionize the world of technology. There are many more examples like the V8 engine, the dream of Henry Ford. When he decided to produce his V8 engine, he asked his engineers to produce a design for the engine, and the engineers told him, 'Sir, it is impossible to produce a V8 engine.' But Mr. Ford responded, 'I want my V8 engine,' and the rest is history.

Dr. K. Anji Reddy envisioned a future with remarkable clarity, inspired by his profound experience witnessing the Pfizer plant during his PhD days in Pune. His dream was very clear: to see his plan after seeing the Pfizer plant. He painted a picture in his mind that one day, my plant would bear the fruits of passion and dedication.

So, what are the key factors crucial for the success of beginning with the end in mind? "Suppose you have a plan to get promoted to the next level in the next three years, so you have to begin with the time frame of 2 years from now. First, you should revisit your past success.

What has brought you here? Which were skills that helped you to get promoted? Are you practicing the same skills or learning new skills? You will require new skills for the next level of Job, and you have to acquire those new skills. Are you doing something about this? If not, start now...

**EXERCISE FOR YOU**

List out your strengths, your aspirations, your key skills, and your achievements.

**My Aspiration:**

_____

My key Skills:

1.

2.

3.

My past achievements-

1.

2.

3.

Now, prepare a list of wants and not of desires; why not desires? Because desires are weak. A few key aspects are as follows: if you are already good at some of them, you should appreciate yourself, and if you have to develop, then make an action plan.

# TIME MANAGEMENT

**Time management is a very crucial skill; it helps you** make the best of your available time; this will enhance your efficiency, and you will achieve your goals effectively. Remember, every day, we all have 24 hours. Still, you find many people say- I don't have time. If I could get more time, etc. Why it happens to them? Because they don't understand the value of time. They don't know how to manage their time. They don't know how to prioritize things to use every minute of their precise life.

What is the value of time?

Imagine the following to understand the real value of time

1- Your friend who failed in class- What is the value of 1 year to him?

2- A mother delivered a baby in 8 months- a premature baby- what is the value of that one month to her?

3- You have to publish a weekly report and need to collect data from different sources- what is the value of 1 week to you?

4- You are going to meet your soulmate after 1 hour- what is the value of that 1 Hour to you?

5- You just missed your train by 1 minute. What is the value of that 1 minute to you?

6- Someone just avoided an accident – it could be a matter of one life to him. And

7- If you were born on the 29th of February, you know the value of 1 day.

Why have I put one day at No 7? You had this thought? Yes, I share your sentiment. One can create lasting memories and cherish every moment effectively by managing that particular day. The key is to make the most of every moment, ensuring that each day becomes an opportunity to celebrate.

There is a valuable lesson to be learned from a story about Warrant Buffet. When asked about his secrets to success, Buffet once shared an insightful anecdote: he handed a reporter a blank cheque and told him to write any amount he desired. The reporter, thinking it was a joke or perhaps not realizing the gravity of the situation, hesitated and missed a golden opportunity. Warren Buffet said- you have just lost a huge opportunity; in my life, I have never missed any opportunity, small or big, and that is the secret of my success.

"Effective time management requires vigilance, preparation, and readiness to seize the opportunity moments as they arise."

The art of managing time requires the following.

**A- Clear Goal Setting.**

**B- Time allocation.**

**C- Stay Focused on the task.**

Review the progress and make course corrections.

Let us understand the Goal Setting in detail.

**Goal Setting**- Goal Setting is a powerful tool for personal growth. You have aspirations, and you have a list of your wants (not Desires), and if you have a clear roadmap, then you can improve yourself. The following are aspects of goal setting –

### 1. SMART GOALS

Your goals should be Specific, Measurable, Achievable/Ambitious, Relevant/Realistic, and Time-bound.

The difference between Achievable and Ambitious.

**Achievable goals** will give you a sense of accomplishment and progress. This always motivates you to build confidence, and **Ambitious goals** will push you to strive for excellence; here, you are more creative and achieve new heights.

**Relevant** means your goals are in line with the bigger picture and vision. **Realistic** refers to something that can be done with available resources. Let me share an example.

You are working as a first-line or front-line Manager in any industry and want to get promoted to a mid-level management position within the next two years. This goal is aligned with your work experience and current skill set, so it is **realistic**.

This goal is **relevant** to your career aspirations and will contribute to your overall professional growth. It is in line with your interest and in the direction you want to take your career.

The following example will clarify more-

**Achievable and Ambitious**: You have a goal to attain a senior leadership role within the next five years. This is achievable while ambitious; it is realistic as you have a solid track record of performance, relevant experience, and a commitment to your personal development. A senior-level leadership position may require additional skills and experience, which you are willing to acquire in that period since it is ambitious. This goal will push you beyond your comfort zone and will require substantial effort and dedication. A new role will bring more responsibility with authority, and you should be ready to accept the responsibility that will come with the authority of the new role.

### 2. LONG-TERM VISION

Goal setting is not just about short-term achievements; it is about creating a long-term vision for your personal growth and professional success.

I am delighted to share the vision of Dr. K Anji Reddy; he could foresee the pharmaceutical sector alleviating suffering and improving lives. His vision was beyond the boundaries of traditional business; it was a vision of creating a healthier world, especially for those who could not afford expensive medications. This deep sense of purpose drove him, and he focused on research and development to innovate and make essential medicines more affordable.

His long-term vision was rooted in the belief that high–quality healthcare should be a fundamental right, not a privilege. His visionary approach to drug development resulted in the production of cost-effective medications that reached millions of people globally.

Dr. K. Anji Reddy's story inspires leaders to see beyond the bottom line; his legacy stands as a beacon, reminding us that true visionary leadership transforms industry and, above all, uplifts humanity.

### 3. PERSONAL DEVELOPMENT GOALS

To be future-ready, your goals must include acquiring new skills and developing emotional intelligence.

**Here are a few points to consider-**

**Improve time management skills** – create a daily schedule with dedicated time slots for work, personal tasks, and relaxation. You must allocate time for small breaks to relax and be ready with more energy.

**Stay fit**- exercise for at least 35 minutes daily.

Improve your communication skills and be confident while communicating with the team.

**Be adaptive to change** - learn from every situation, including unexpected situations.

**Keep a work-life balance**- Rule: allocate time for work, for family, for yourself, and don't break the rule.

**Continuous Learning**- acquire new skills that are relevant to your career.

**Improve your Networking-** especially with professionals in your field.

**Cultivate mindfulness-** develop a habit of meditating for a few minutes daily, and this will reduce your stress and enhance focus.

### 4. POSITIVE AFFIRMATIONS

This is very powerful. You must include positive affirmations, which will help you develop a positive mindset. This will help you develop confidence in your ability to achieve your set goals. I am sharing a few examples; I suggest saying these affirmations for 5 minutes daily in the morning and 5 minutes before bedtime.

a- I am a skilled professional and can overcome any challenges.

b- I attract success with every interaction.

c- I am a master at building rapport and establishing trust.

d- I lead with positivity, motivating and inspiring my team to achieve their best.

e- I am a confident and capable leader, making sound decisions for the benefit of my team and organization.

### 5. ADAPTABILITY

Life is changing fast, and there may be new and difficult scenarios, so be flexible and ready to accept change. We will talk more about adaptability in a later chapter.

### 6. CELEBRATIONS

develop a habit of celebrating small successes; this will help you to motivate yourself, and you will provide an opportunity for self-reflection.

Share your Goals with your mentor and maybe with your family and team members whom you can trust. Also, share your growth with them; they will encourage you to do better.

### 7. LEARN FROM MISTAKES

learn from each experience and take it as an opportunity to learn more. Make a proper analysis of what went wrong, make new plans to do better, and never repeat the same mistake.

### 8. HAVE WORK AND PERSONAL LIFE BALANCE

Regularly visit and revisit your goals, see the progress, and revise the plan as your priorities and circumstances change.

This habit will foster continuous personal growth and development.

# OPPORTUNITY ASSESSMENT AND MANAGEMENT

## UNDERSTAND YOUR PROBLEM

Some people are good at identifying opportunities but need help managing them, so as an effective leader, you have to manage them as well.

I met a young dentist in a big city. and he shared the following with me.

I had a passion for identifying opportunities and turning them into successful ventures. I see opportunities everywhere, and people ignore these opportunities. One day (during my college days), I was walking through a local market, and I noticed a growing trend of health-conscious consumers looking for unique and nutritious food options. Recognizing this as an opportunity, I started searching and discovering an ancient grain that was not only healthy but also sustainable and versatile. I decided to start a business centered around this grain. I started this business with my clinic, and I faced various challenges. I spent more time seeing the market size and competition; I spoke to many nutritionists in the city and also discussed with many storekeepers who were selling such items. By doing this exercise, I could find out the gap and need for ready–to–eat products made from ancient grain. I saw the opportunity to see the product to create healthy snacks and meals that would appeal to the busy urban lifestyle. I was very clear about the opportunity in my mind; I moved to the next step. It was about assessment and management. Potential risks, for example, changes in consumer preferences, how to manage supply, margins, stock inventory, etc. I made a plan and also a plan B. I discussed my plan with one of my friends and had a strategic partnership. I launched the product with Gym first and got instant success.  I encountered a new challenge that I had not expected in the beginning: the sudden spike in the cost of that grain. Since my friend was an experienced person, he negotiated long-term contracts with suppliers and could manage this crisis well. Today, his business is doing well, and so is his practice.  This is an example of opportunity assessment and its management. There is risk; there is the reward. So do proper research and make a perfect plan.

**Problem-Solving Solutions and not only problems – by practicing this, you can also** respect your leader's time and do your part the best.

Some people see the problem everywhere and in everything, and in the same society, you find people who have solutions for such people's problems. They know the problem is subjective and context-dependent.

During my childhood, I visited my relative's place for summer vacation. It was the last week of June, and the heat was unbearable. People were praying for rain. One day, it finally started raining, and it was a fun experience for children my age. However, the rain became heavier, and within a few hours, it turned into a minor flood. The water level started to rise, causing the villagers to gather at a particular location.

Some were discussing the potential damage, while one villager proposed a plan to prevent the damage to their houses and fields.

In the same village lived a man named Ramdas, who had an optimistic outlook. Despite the situation, he saw an opportunity in the rain. He believed that there were blessings in disguise and that the fields needed the water to flourish. Ramdas suggested that the village should celebrate by playing music and singing songs since everyone was already gathered in one place. He saw it as a chance to celebrate the unity of the villagers. Ramdas reminded everyone that the problem was temporary and that there could be hidden benefits after that.

Eventually, the villagers understood the subjective nature of the problem and learned that there is always a silver lining in every situation. Ask for help and feedback- Reach out to your leader and ask for his feedback and suggestions on your strengths and areas of improvement.

## UNDERSTAND YOUR COMMUNICATION

As you know, effective communication extends beyond words alone. you can communicate with words, without words (Body Language), and with the impactful tone of voice. Master the art of being a confident communicator.

It becomes very important for a leader to be a good communicator, and to be a good communicator, it is equally important to be a good listener. The leader has many challenges, and sometimes the situation itself is difficult; there is a crisis, and the leader has to communicate with the team;

his challenge is – how can he keep transparency, how he builds trust, how can he gain confidence in the team, and so on. Some leaders are committed and keep open and honest communication with the team even when delivering challenging news. It reminds me of one such leader.

The company decided to close its operations in India as the company was facing financial challenges. The news broke in the air and created uncertainty. There was anxiety in the people, which affected their morale and overall productivity. The leadership team understood the importance of transparent communication but faced challenges in communicating difficult news still while maintaining morale and trust. There was a need for a strategy to communicate openly and honestly. Senior management decided to share this difficult news with his core team instead of denying it or covering it jo till the announcement was made public.

The CEO decided to share early with the team, and he also shared the challenges the company was facing. He made sure to share the updates with the team regularly so people were well informed. He also encouraged people to share their concerns and ideas. The situation was tough, but this openness has reduced some anxiety in the team. The advantage of such open communication was that some people could make their decision to support their family with other options. Even in such a challenging situation, people appreciated the openness of the CEO. This contributed to maintaining a level of trust and morale within the organization. This approach has helped the CEO minimize the negative impact of rumors and people engaged in company operations. Afterward, the company underwent an acquisition by another organization, and the CEO reassured all employees that they would seamlessly transition into the new system without encountering any challenges.

This case is an example of open communication that has helped the CEO build trust, maintain the morale of employees, and keep them engaged. His approach facilitated a smoother transition.

Sharpen your Axe - Read books on self-help. I have explained key elements in my book, "THE ONE THING." You can find more books. Attend a live seminar/workshop if you have time constraints.

Why is it so important? Because complacency can be a roadblock to sustained success. Your past accomplishments will not guarantee you success in the future, so to remain relevant, you must upgrade your learning, learn new skills, acquire new knowledge, put this knowledge into action, and help your team to deliver better, and your team will push you upward.

You can have a strategy to upgrade yourself. there are few options as

Continuous learning - stay committed to learning by reading books and attending seminars, online courses, and live workshops. Stay informed about emerging trends.

Networking- recognize the importance of networking, learn from your peers and their experiences, and share your experience with others.

Mentorship- this will surely help you to keep yourself ahead of others. Mentorship will provide you with invaluable insights, guidance, and a broader perspective on industry challenges.

New skills or new technology- be open to learning new skills and keep updated with new developments in the field of technology.

Be Creative and Innovative – the good news is that you can be creative and innovative in your routine activities, too. Be open to change, and keep experimenting.

Be Positive- Like attracts like, and this will work as a catalyst, and you can bring positivity to your workplace. Remember, Positivity is not merely a state of mind; it is a powerful force that propels us forward, even in challenging situations. As we journey from strength to strength, positivity acts as a lighthouse, guiding us through the stormy waters of life. When we cultivate a positive mindset, we develop the ability to transform obstacles into opportunities and setbacks into comebacks. So let positivity be the ink that colors the stories of your life. Start believing in yourself and say- **every challenge is an opportunity for growth.**

### STORY #1

Let me share the story of Soichiro Honda, founder of one of the biggest automobile manufacturing companies in the world; today, they have a presence in more than 140 countries. His story is very inspiring. I am sharing a few things about him here. Mr Honda was from a small village in Japan, and his father was running a bicycle shop. He was assisting his father in his business. Though he was from a small village, he always had big DREAMS. He was a curious child and attracted to making new things. Though he was an average student, he had an interest in practicals, so he left his studies early in his life after seeing an advertisement in the newspaper about a need for some mechanics for the Art Shokai company. He made a big decision to leave his village and go to Tokyo for that job.

He got the job, but being the youngest employee, he was given small tasks like an intern instead of the junior mechanic job he expected. He did not want to return to his village, so he accepted that job. Despite doing small tasks, he kept learning and improving his skills with motor mechanics. He continued to learn and to improve his knowledge and skills in motor machines. The owner noticed his dedication to learning and started teaching Soichiro business-related matters. His hard work paid off the dividend, and he was promoted to the position of branch manager when he was 22 years old.

His passion was for creating significant innovations, so he eventually left that position. he learned the ropes and ventured into making piston rings. Despite an initial struggle, he succeeded in producing top–quality piston rings, which gained recognition from companies like Toyota. Everything was going smoothly until a shock hit – the war with China began. Facing a shortage of skilled workers who left for the war, Mr. Honda turned this challenge into an opportunity.

He simplified the procedure to make them more straightforward, even the female employees ( as most of the male employees had left for the war) to handle the tasks efficiently. Things started to improve, but then another significant shock came his way. During the war, his factory was destroyed by bombs, but he didn't give up. He believed in himself and his dreams. With strong determination, he quickly gathered the strength to start over. He created a new company called "Honda Motors," focusing on making motorcycles instead of the piston rings he used to make.

His company became a leading motorcycle company. Later, he wanted to make Cars, but the department rejected his idea, giving many reasons. However, he didn't let setbacks stop him. He worked hard and created an efficient car model that everyone liked, and the department approved it. Very soon, Honda became a famous name among car users.

Do you find his story inspiring?

Can you identify a few of his strengths?

Which strength do you want to develop?

**MUST TAKE INITIATIVE**

It can be small even, but your team members and leader must notice it.

We used to have weekly meetings with my team and were using hard copies for review; a junior colleague, not even a confirmed employee, suggested we make a soft copy that can be used as a running sheet and, in the end, should have a complete report for the month.

I liked his idea, and he developed a new format that was very useful and easy to use. He did it after his routine work; his efforts were small, but the impact was big.

**BE INNOVATIVE**

Innovation does not mean discovering new. It already exists, but you are doing it differently and bringing better results. In simple terms, Innovation means continuous improvement.

Let us remember the transformative power of innovation. It will help you to imagine the solution to your problems. Think beyond boundaries. Keep innovating and stay ahead of the competition, and this will have a lasting impact. So formula is

**Strength + Positivity + Innovation = Growth and Lasting Impact**

Example: If you want a promotion within your organization!!

What is Important?

Does your leader know that you want to be promoted? Are you adding value to your current role? Are you making meaningful contributions during internal team meetings? Like – Review meetings, Monthly meetings, New Product launch meetings, etc.

You must prepare well and plan perfectly.

Remember- Perfect planning prevents poor performance.

# PLAN WELL

**WHAT IS PLANNING?**

"Planning" is the most crucial element of any action. It is the process of turning your idea into reality. Planning can be of three types: strategic, operational, and tactical.

Strategic planning involves determining your goals and objectives.

It is a roadmap that will guide you to achieve your objectives step by step and also help you think about why at every step you take. It is a powerful guide that will help you align your team, resources, and efforts toward a shared vision. It is a foundation on which you will build your tactical and operational plan.

Tactical planning, on the other hand, means defining goals and figuring out how to achieve them. It's important to remember that talent is important, but tact is essential in tactical planning. It is the bridge between strategy and action. So, you need to outline the responsibilities and set a timeline for each action, and at the same time, key performance parameters need to be in place.

Operational planning comes after strategic planning and involves creating a detailed roadmap. In operational planning, you set timelines for each action, assign roles, set milestones, and determine who will do what. You also need to analyze the resources required to execute your plan. Operational plans take tactical initiatives and translate them into daily action.

You are holding a key position in the organization and have responsibilities to ensure the organization's vision is going to be achieved by the daily actions of your team. So day to day operations has to be aligned with strategy and clear vision.

### STORY #1

I am sharing a story from my childhood. I was a small boy living in a small village that did not have electricity or roads and relied on hand pumps and wells for water. I witnessed great unity among the villagers during any festival or occasion. They were supportive of each other, and I miss those things today.

One January, a marriage ceremony was planned for the second week of February, and villagers were planning it together. The villagers sourced milk from their cows and buffalos to support the family of the bride. However, Ramdas asked a genuine question about what would happen if it rained that day. This question brought seriousness to the face of many villagers, as there was no plan for such an event.

Ramdas took responsibility and collected money from everyone to arrange for materials that might be needed. He agreed with the shopkeeper that if they didn't use the materials, he would get a full refund. Ramdas also suggested that people cut down on sweet items but spare milk as people would require hot tea more than sweet.

Ramdas organized everything, including decoration, and was in charge of everything. He had notes in his diary for everything, including collecting keys from the headmaster of the school in case it rained. Ramdas managed everything nicely with a small budget, and with the help of his friends, he decorated the stage in style. This event was a benchmark for all future events.

On the final day, he managed every program quite well, and his efforts were endless. It was early morning the next day, and it started raining, but Ramdas had a plan. He managed the situation so well that even today, people talk about his leadership quality.

I learned a few things that day, and I am sharing what I learned. Ramdas selected the venue and even thought of what would be best in case it rained. He created a checklist with a contingency plan. Arranged material (Resources) as per his plan, allocated resources, and divided tasks among his friends

He took responsibility and led from the front.

In professional life, planning is key as well. For example, if you are doing sales planning or working on marketing plans, then you can follow and use what you have learned.

Remember – you will get what you want!

**EXERCISE FOR YOU**

Which strengths do you have?

1.

2.

3.

What are your Aspirations?

1.  (You have already had)

2.

3.

# WHAT IS GOOD AND WHAT IS NOT

Ramdas went to his Guru Ji and expressed his confusion. He had learned many things from his Guru and from his own experiences about what is good and what is not, but he noticed that what he once considered good needed to be clarified to him. He asked his Guru why this was so.

Upon hearing this, Guru Ji smiled and offered Ramdas a glass of buttermilk. Guru Ji asked Ramdas to hold the glass while he poured the buttermilk into it. Ramdas was glad to drink something refreshing after feeling quite exhausted.

As Guru Ji poured the buttermilk, Ramdas focused on the glass, making sure that there was no wastage. As the glass filled up, Ramdas expected Guru Ji to stop pouring, but he did not. When the glass was full, Ramdas told Guru Ji that the glass could not hold any more buttermilk and that it would overflow. At that moment, Guru Ji stopped pouring and asked Ramdas if he had found his answer. Confused, Ramdas inquired where the answer was. Guru Ji smiled and explained that just as Ramdas' mind was like a full glass and could not accommodate anything new, he needed to empty his mind to make room for new ideas and learning. Ramdas was feeling better but was not fully convinced. He said Guru Ji, Yesterday was very good, and everything was fine, but today, life is full of trouble, and nothing good is happening to me. Guru Ji took Ramdas to a pond and asked him to pick up a small stone and throw it into the water. As the stone hit the surface, it created ripples that disturbed the otherwise calm waters. Guru Ji then explained to Ramdas that life can be compared to this pond; while yesterday may have been calm and undisturbed like the pond's surface, today, a small change, like throwing a stone, can create many ripples. However, with time, the ripples will settle down, and the surface of the pond will become calm again. Guru Ji advised Ramdas to be patient and wait, as life will also return to its calm state after a period of turbulence.

**Are you facing such ripples in your life? Wait, it will settle -down itself –Soon!**

Nature maintains a balance, and what is considered good or bad depends on the situation and circumstances. Society accepts what is good and rejects what is not. Guru Ji believed that helping others without prioritizing one's interests was a good deed. However, helping others by putting oneself first might not be considered good. There are numerous examples around us where the actions taken may be ethically or morally right but legally wrong. Yet, we still feel good about doing them. For example – Jumping a red signal is wrong, but if you are helping a lady with labor pain and jump the red signal, even after paying a penalty, you feel good.

### INFORMATION OR IGNORANCE

**Information is the key to success- and Ignorance is Sin**

I asked many people in my life and tried to get the answer to my question—

What is the key to Success? Different people gave different answers, and I am sharing a few of them here.

- Happiness is the key to success

- Knowledge is the key to success

- Action is key to success, and someone added that perseverance is that action.

- Focusing on the goal is key to success

- Failure is key to success

- Patience is key to success

- Motivation is the key to success

- Ambition is key to success

- Practice is key to success

I have a memory from years ago when I asked my father a question about success. He replied by asking me a question in return. His question was, "Who will decide about your success?" My response was, it is me and not someone else. His second question to me was- what is the key to success for me and why?

I answered that the key to success is information. However, my father offered a different perspective. He said that having information is one thing, but not using it is another. I then suggested that using information is the key to success. However, my father asked me another question, "In which situation and with what information?" I was unsure how to answer, as everything sounded right to me. Then, he explained that success is in relative terms, and people compare themselves to others to determine who is more successful. His suggestion was simple and very clear: Don't allow people to judge your success. Second, know your motive and take action in time.

I didn't understand, so I asked him to explain it to me. In response to my request, he said...**MOTIVe+AcTION.**

If you are clear about your motive, then you will acquire the right information that you can use to fulfill it. And will use that information to take action.

So, information is key to success if used properly at the right time. Not only this, but information opens the door to new opportunities and insights.in today's fast-changing world, staying informed is not merely a choice but an absolute necessity. Knowledge empowers individuals to make informed decisions.

Ignorance can be linked to sin, as it closes the door to understanding and hinders the ability to make positive contributions.

So, the path to success is to develop a mindset that values continuous learning and sees out new information.

"I asked about failure and was told that it should never be considered final if you refuse to accept it. Failure can actually make you stronger and better prepared for future attempts, giving you more confidence. Therefore, it is important to develop a never-give-up attitude. Every failure is a learning experience that can help you grow as a person. So, don't be afraid of failure, but rather use it as an opportunity to learn from your mistakes and avoid repeating them in the future". What about happiness? I asked my father, and his response was;

When do you feel happy? When I do something that I like. I said to him.

He said you are right because **Happiness** has a profound effect on our minds.

I have made it clearer now, and you will get clearer by going through the following research.

**Anchor's** research has proven that increasing happiness can reduce stress by over 23%, improve health by 39%, and increase productivity by 31%. Happy people tend to be more creative, better problem-solvers, and take initiative. So, it's important to maintain a positive attitude toward life, even when negativity surrounds us. Positive individuals tend to lead happier, more successful lives, bring better results, and develop good teams around them. I've learned that even 5-minute positive affirmations or self-talk can help you stay positive. It's important always to use positive words when talking to yourself. For example, saying, "Today I am feeling better, "I am the best, "I can do it," It's a very nice atmosphere today," "I am successful," "I am strong," "I am more confident" are all good examples of positive affirmations. Smile a little more- it will help you to stay positive.

In the beginning, you may find it a little difficult because negative thoughts may come in between, but your never-give-up attitude will not allow negative thoughts to occupy any place in your mind.

It's important to be assertive without being aggressive. Assertive behavior helps you stay confident and avoid stress. Let's examine the benefits of being assertive. Let me share what my father told me about happiness-

He said- happiness is not avoiding challenges or pretending everything is perfect. It is all about the small moments that bring a smile to your face. If you can bring a smile to the faces of others, then you can bring desired changes in this society. But remember- you can give what you have!! He used to share the story of Walt Disney with us to prepare us for a better future by staying positive. He used to say- don't expect success to come overnight and have - a never-give-up attitude; Walt Disney himself was rejected over 300 times before Mickey Mouse became a super hit. Learn from mistakes (others' mistakes) and be more creative.

### ASSERTIVENESS

Assertive people can protect their self-esteem and also help others enhance their self-esteem. Being assertive means, you respect yourself and show respect to others. You always use positive words in assertive behavior. Assertive people always set high standards for themselves.

Assertive people have self-awareness; they know their strengths and areas of improvement, and they are willing to change and improve. They listen to others with respect.

When you offer an Idea or suggestion- it is assertiveness.

When you are polite, and I say I'm afraid I have to disagree with your point- it is assertiveness.

When you give your opinion and ask about your opinion (you say- How you feel)- it is assertiveness.

When you say No and you do not feel guilty –it is assertiveness.

So, be assertive and practice assertiveness.

It's important to avoid arrogance, as it can cause you to lose control over your thoughts, lack direction, and move away from success. Aggressive people often suffer from a superiority complex and are poor listeners, thinking they know everything. They tend to judge others quickly and cannot see their weaknesses while exaggerating their strengths.

It reminds me of one experience that I had during the final round of my job interview for a senior-level position. The director of the organization expressed his concern before handing over the offer letter to me and said, Gentleman, I am happy and impressed with your overall presentation. Still, my only concern is that you don't seem to be aggressive. Then, how will you drive the team for results?

My response to him, with all respect to his position, was -

Assertiveness is a strength to communicate clearly and effectively. It has the power to turn a potential conflict into opportunities for collaboration and understanding. Assertiveness is not about being loud or forceful. It is about how confidently you are expressing yourself and standing up for what you believe in. An assertive person will always maintain control over his thoughts and language.

He was satisfied with my approach, and I, with my team, delivered the best results for the organization. One must practice Assertiveness, and there is no need to be aggressive every time.

**EXERCISE FOR YOU**

A)  List some of the qualities you have in you.

1

2.

3.

B)  What are areas where you want to work on being an assertive person?

1.

2.

3.

# BEING EMPATHETIC

Is there anything more required than being assertive? You are right. Being assertive is one thing, and you need more than just being assertive. Some of the keywords are:

**Empathy, Accountability, Innovation, Inspiration, Adaptability, communication, and team building are a few to mention here.**

### EMPATHY

Empathy is very important to build on your strengths; empathy is the ability to see things from another person's perspective. Being empathetic means you can see the emotions of other people, and you can imagine the feeling of another person. Imagine you are in a meeting and you are giving full attention to someone, showing genuine interest in him and showing your curiosity to know more about his achievements, his life, his success, his troubles, etc, also providing constructive feedback. This means you are showing empathy to his person.

As shared by one of my friends.

One day, while working in Delhi with my colleague who is from Bihar, he received a call from his hometown informing him about his grandmother's ill health. He was very upset as he was very close to her, and she had taken care of him during his childhood. He insisted on leaving immediately to be with his grandmother. I tried to assure him that she would be all right, but he was adamant about leaving. I then called one of our managers and explained the situation to him, requesting him to assist our colleague's father and ensure that his grandmother received the best possible treatment at a good hospital.

Meanwhile, I took my colleague to a restaurant to console him. He was concerned about meeting customers as I had come from the head office. I advised him not to worry and that we would meet the customers after having a cup of coffee at the restaurant. After about 45 minutes, I received a call from my colleague's father, who informed me that my manager had been an angel to him. He had taken my mother to the best hospital in his car, and she had received timely treatment. She was recovering fast, and the diagnosis had been made. The doctor had suggested a few more tests that would be done soon. I handed the phone to my colleague and suggested that he can go to his home now. However, his father insisted that his mother was feeling better and that she would rest at home. He advised his son not to worry and come later when he could get a confirmed train ticket.

I appreciated my colleague for his decision, and this is an excellent example of empathy.

### ACCOUNTABILITY

What is accountability? It is different than being responsible.

Responsibility refers to the obligation to complete a task. For instance, if you work in sales, it is your responsibility to achieve your sales target. In order to achieve your target, it is important to meet your customers in a timely manner and provide them with accurate information. Responsibility can be shared or delegated among multiple individuals.

Accountability, on the other hand, pertains to being answerable for the success or failure of a project, task, or goal. If you are accountable, you have the authority and power to make decisions. Accountability cannot be shared or delegated.

In essence, responsibility is about fulfilling assigned tasks or roles, while accountability is about answering for the overall success or failure of a project or objective. In many situations, accountability is a higher-level concept that encompasses responsibility. In a well-functioning team or organization, individuals may be responsible for various tasks, but there is often someone who is ultimately accountable for the project's success.

### STORY #1

In my village, there was a marriage function, and people helped each other carry out activities in a way that there was absolute harmony and everything was done in time. People used to make plates with leaves from local trees. The task of preparing plates was assigned to a group of people. Unfortunately, there was rain, and the group could not complete the task in time. There was a quash, and people were blaming others, and someone was giving credit to God for untimely rains. No one was willing to come forward and provide a solution to the family. In this tense situation, Ramdas came forward and gathered some talented boys and motivated them by giving them responsibility by saying only you can do it. It is a matter of our village's reputation. Let us collect leaves and dry them with the help of fire. We will do the job for an extra hour and will make sure that we have enough plates before the function. The team did a wonderful job, and Ramdas gave them full credit.

Remember – Accountability is going beyond your responsibility.

**INNOVATION**

What is innovation?

Innovation is a continuous process of improvement, and it doesn't necessarily have to involve a discovery. You can innovate in various aspects of your business, such as your product, process, or approach to customer service. By innovating, you can increase your efficiency and effectiveness in achieving your sales objectives, which, in turn, can lead to improved customer satisfaction.

Innovation in the sales process means staying ahead of the competition by finding creative ways to meet customers' needs, for example, by using digital platforms to reach your customers. This can help you improve your sales forecasting and inventory management, minimize losses, and improve overall profitability for your organization.

Suppose I have to quote one name that can be an excellent example of Innovation. In that case, the name will be Dr. K. Anji Reddy, founder, and chairman of Dr.Reddy's Laboratories, who played a pivotal role in bringing innovation to the Indian pharmaceutical industry. One notable example of his innovation is his role in the development of bulk Drug manufacturing in India. In the early 80s, India had a huge dependency on the import of bulk drugs, and as a result, it was a very costly affair. His efforts and innovation helped the country become a significant player in the global pharmaceutical industry. This approach has helped to make essential medicines cost-effective for the Indian population.

**STORY #2**

Let me take you back to my village and my childhood.

We had a pond in the corner of my village, and the source of water for animals, but the problem was during peak months of hot summer like June. During the heat at its peak, the pond usually gets dried, and villagers used to face difficulty in providing water to their animals. Ramdas thought of a brilliant idea at no extra cost, and he solved two problems. He called a meeting in my house as people used to listen to my father with great respect, so he used that platform and threw an idea. Ramdas said, I have been to another village and saw the streets were more beautiful and clean than our village. So, as usual, there are people who see the problem first, so they say it will cost money, who will give money, etc. Ramdas said, I have gathered information, and it is done by themselves, and people have worked without money. It is not possible, according to some of them. My father understood the motive behind this and asked Ramdas to share his experience. Ramdas was excited to share his idea. He said Guru Ji, people in that village had agreed to take care of the street only in front of their house individually but as a team, and everyone had taken the mud from their village only, so they had to pay nothing to anyone. Everyone was so excited and decided to start the work immediately. In the next 15 days, the streets were beautiful with proper elevation from the current level, so the problem of waterlogging was solved, but the major issue was resolved permanently. The pond was dug by over 2 feet, and the capacity to hold water in the pond was increased. The next year, people had enough water in the pond till it rained.

What an Innovative idea!

**INSPIRATION**

- Motivate and uplift your team through your actions and words. Identify the motive of each team member and encourage them to take action.

- Build a strong and respectful team.

- Have clear goal

- Be genuinely interested in team members and appreciate their efforts. Support them to be successful.

- Take responsibility. Don't believe in excuses. Don't blame others.

- Set clear personal goals and help the team set clear goals for success.

- Be with them in their ups and downs.

- Built a culture of trust. The best example I can share with you here-

**Dalai Lama said-**, "If you feel a sense of concern for the well-being of others, then trust will come.

Sometimes, small incidents give you big lessons; some inspire you, some motivate you, and others teach you values. Let me share a few such examples, and you can decide about- Inspiration and value.

I was in an important meeting with my L& D Director and was deciding the contents for the workshop for leaders in middle management; this was very important as the company gave us the mandate to identify future leaders so we could design development plans for their grooming.

In the meantime, his phone rang; he disconnected it, and it rang again; his response was the same. When the phone rang a third time, I said, Sir, please take a call; it may be urgent. His response was as follows.

Nothing is more important than the agenda that we have in hand; if there is something urgent, then the call can come again, but I can not ask you to hold. I learned the lesson that day. A person who is with you deserves more time than the person who is calling you over the phone.

This happens around us every day, and sometimes we make such mistakes. Let us avoid this in the future.

My Sales Head shared another incident. His daughter joined a company in Hyderabad, and he gave her a mobile phone to connect with her family (in those days, mobiles were not very common and calling was very costly). He got a call from a landline number, as it was very common, so he picked up the call and said Hello. He heard the voice that said at the other end it was his daughter, so the question was, have you lost your mobile? NO was the response from the other side; his second question was, why are you calling from a landline number? Is it a PCO center? The response from her daughter was no, Dad, it is my office number. He disconnected the call immediately and dialed her number to give a message that he never used company property for personal use.

Is this not inspiring stories? We get great value from such experiences. I feel proud to be part of such a team that had such great leaders.

### ADAPTABILITY

*Adaptability is about the powerful difference between adapting to cope and adapting to win- Max McKeown.*

Adaptability is the key that will open the door of possibilities. Adaptability is your ability to adjust to new conditions and changes. Today the world is changing very fast and so are your circumstances hence you must be ready to adapt to new conditions.

If you can adapt to change fast, you will transform the challenges into opportunities for your success. Adaptability is more than a skill; it is a mindset, so you have to embrace these changes and adjust fast. Life is full of uncertainties and mysteries; you don't know what it will be like tomorrow.

Today, you are enjoying a good relationship with your seniors and have a very cordial relationship. You are performing, and suddenly, there can be changes, and you don't know what will happen tomorrow. So, always be ready for change and develop a mindset to adapt to change.

Once you are working as a team leader and you are responsible for building a team and a culture of performance, in that situation, this adaptability will work like glue and help you bind your team together. The advantage of this mindset is that it will help you get new ideas, people will cooperate in a better way, and you will bring innovation and creativity to your workplace.

Here are a few real-life examples of individuals showcasing adaptability.

Elon Musk, the co-founder of PayPal, which was later sold to eBay, is a classic example of adaptability in the business world. He went on to establish Tesla Motors, SpaceX, SolarCity, and more. His ability to transition from online payments to electric cars and renewable energy is remarkable.

Steve Jobs, the late co-founder of Apple, was a master of adaptability in the tech industry. His remarkable ability to understand the market needs and innovate products as per market demands made him an icon in the industry. Another example is Kiran Mazumdar Shaw. Her ability to adapt to the evolving landscape of biotechnology and her persistence in building a successful company has made her not only one of the most influential businesswomen in India but also a role model for aspiring entrepreneurs.

## STORY #3

As a front-line Manager with a well-known Pharmaceutical company, I was based in Western Uttar Pradesh. However, I received my first transfer to the Eastern part of the State, a city I had never been to before. While I was confident, my family was worried about my living arrangements and food. I reassured them that everything would be all right. After I joined the new HQ, my team performed well, and I received another transfer to a new city in the same part of the state. I applied all my learnings from the previous transfer and achieved success in my new role as well.

During an event, one of my colleagues asked me which city I liked the most. I responded with Allahabad (now known as Prayagraj), but another colleague reminded me that I had previously said it was Varanasi. I acknowledged that they were right, as I had been based in Varanasi at that time. This situation can be considered an apt example of adaptability.

### COMMUNICATION

*I liked a quote by Jeffrey Morales, CEO of California High-Speed Rail Authority. He said- "communicate respectfully – don't just tell your team members what you want, but explain to them why."*

You will agree that there is a world of difference between telling and selling.

Telling is one way, but selling involves understanding the needs, challenges, and concerns of the other person. Always focus on selling, not telling.

As you know, selling is an art and a science, and therefore, effective communication requires a high level of skill. The good news is that you can develop this skill by practicing. Use this skill to build a strong relationship with the team by fostering a culture of collaboration.

Talk with clarity, be respectful while speaking to the team, listen to them with respect, and show genuine interest in them to understand their true emotions.

As a leader, when you are communicating with a team, it is your responsibility to make them understand the purpose of your communication; it is possible if you are prepared well and are precise in your talk. Choose your words carefully so they do not hurt others, and avoid unnecessary jargon.

Convert your communication into a powerful tool that will leave a positive impact on your team.

Effective Communication will help to

A) Built trust and create a strong bond with your team.

B) Enhance your credibility as a leader.

C) C-Express a clear and inspiring vision.

Leaders who communicate transparently create an environment where everyone is informed, engaged, and aligned with the organization's direction.

In my book "The One Thing," I have shared one experience, and the learning from that experience is- "Think like an

Intelligent person but communicate in the language people understand."

# TEAM BUILDING

*If everyone is moving forward together, then success takes care of itself.* Henry Ford ·

Team building is of paramount importance. Alone, you can achieve a little, but together, we can achieve a lot.

Team building activities always help team members to share their ideas and thoughts effectively. It also encourages open communication.

High-performing teams have strong interpersonal relationships.

Team building activities provide opportunities for team members to connect on a personal level.

Team building activities help improve the morale of the team and bring better results because such activities can make the workplace a fun place where people enjoy doing their best.

Team building activities have a long-lasting positive effect, and there will be such a nice experience where people sort out their differences themselves.

It is proven that team-building activities always help the team generate innovative solutions for even tough problems, and they can solve any problem by brainstorming among themselves.

At this point, you can think of more advantages of team-building exercises. You can identify the strengths and areas of improvement of your team members. You can assign tasks based on their strength to enhance productivity. Enhancing productivity will bring a sense of achievement and will improve employee retention. And team building will foster a culture of adaptability.

So, I believe in investing in team-building activities. Team building will help you to have a better-motivated team, a better work culture, and, above all, a performing team.

### STORY #1

When I think back to my childhood, I still remember learning about teamwork for the first time. It was during my brother's wedding preparations when my father took me along to book a band. The bandmaster gave my father a choice of 9, 11, 15, or more players for my brother's party. Being a curious child, I asked the bandmaster about the difference in the number of players. He explained that the only difference was the number of players playing the same instrument. He then shared an experience where he had led a team of 21 people at a wedding, but 6 of them were new to the group, and they needed more time to rehearse. Despite having a large team, the performance could have been better due to better coordination. He emphasized the importance of having skilled, enthusiastic team members who are coordinated and supportive of each other. He added that even if a team member is less skilled or new, an instructor should help them so that there is perfect harmony and the audience enjoys the music. When I asked him what made his band a star band, he said that the key is perfect synchronization, where the audience cannot distinguish between the individual contributions of each team member.

Is it that easy to build a team? What can help you to build a high-performing team? I learned a lesson from that bandmaster that day. The team is of significant importance in achieving the organization's goal, so team building is a very important role of a leader.

Team building activities are like the heartbeat of organizational success. As we learned from the story above, a team's effort, coordination, and synchronization can determine not only the journey but also the destination. Developing a high-performing team is essential for enduring success.

Team building is not just about having a good time together; it is the foundation for a great organization. A good team means open communication, exchanging ideas, appreciating each other, and creating an atmosphere where everyone feels valued. A good team is a group of people full of creativity and innovation who view challenges as opportunities.

Building such a team can be challenging. You will face interpersonal conflicts, communication breakdowns, and resistance to change. However, these are opportunities for you to prove your skills as a master architect. You know how to overcome these challenges. Effective team building requires a strategic approach. Set clear goals, have open communication, involve everyone, ask for their opinions, encourage them, appreciate their efforts, and have team-building activities like games or workshops to foster trust and collaboration. This way, your workplace can become a second home for them. So I can say – that team building activities are like a good investment that gives you dividends in the currency of collaboration, innovation, and shared success.

A strong and performing team means – a guarantee for sustained success.

Self-reflection can help you to develop a high-performing team, so let us talk about self-reflection.

# SELF -REFLECTION

*"Your best gets better with the right people"- Bill Gates.*

**UNDERSTANDING SELF-REFLECTION**

What is self–reflection?

In simple terms, self-reflection is a process of evaluation and examination of self-thoughts, feelings, and actions. It involves introspection, self-awareness, and your willingness to learn from your own experience. It is very important for your personal growth and development.

Why is self-reflection so important for a leader?

Effective leadership begins with introspection. Through self-reflection, leaders gain clarity, humility, and strength to guide authentically.

Surround yourself with the right people and build a team that inspires each other.

Self-reflection is the beginning of personal growth. It involves a conscious examination of one's values, goals, and beliefs. By gaining a deeper understanding of oneself, individuals can identify areas for improvement and set meaningful objectives.

The following key points will help to understand the importance of self-reflection.

1. Decision Making- Self-reflection will work like a true advisor and will guide you to make a decision that will prove a productive decision in the future.

2. Aligning with your values- introspection can help you ensure your actions align with your core values, creating harmony between your actions and personal beliefs.

3. Continuous Learning and Adaptability- Engaging in self-reflection fosters a growth mindset, enabling one to seize every learning opportunity and adapt to change.

4. Emotional Intelligence- you will improve your communication with others because you will understand the emotions of other people/team members. This approach will strengthen your interpersonal relationship skills.

5. Goal setting and Progress monitoring- Self-reflection will work like a guiding principle and will help you set meaningful and realistic goals. You will review the progress periodically and make necessary corrections in between, which will yield good results.

6. Cultivation of mindfulness- the biggest advantage of self-reflection is that it will help you to be fully present in the moment.

**HOW IT HELPS?**

Self-reflection will help you in your personal and professional development.

I recall a former colleague of mine at Dr Reddy's Laboratories who was always enthusiastic, hardworking, and ambitious. He never shied away from challenges and always strived for success. However, after some time, signs of burnout became evident in him. He was exhausted and stressed out. It was then that we had a discussion, and he decided to engage in some self-reflection.

A few days later, I met him again, and I noticed that he was a completely different person. When I asked him about the secret behind his transformation, he shared that he had asked himself the following questions:

1. What is the one thing that I like most about my job?

2. Which factors are causing me stress?

3. What can I do differently to achieve a better work-life balance?

He began to prioritize his tasks, openly discuss his workload with his team members, and delegate tasks to others so that he wasn't doing everything himself. This process of self-reflection helped him find a better balance and brought out the best in him.

**EXERCISE FOR YOU**

Imagine you are going to a review meeting. Your team has yet to deliver up to your expectations, and you are under pressure to deliver the numbers. You know this is a common problem, and different people have different approaches in such a situation. I suggest having a better self-reflection next time if you have any such situation.

1- Take time and think

    A- Is it a performance issue

    B- Is it a people-related issue

    C- is it a process-related issue

2- Evaluate each situation and take deep breaths.

3- Give serious thought to your behavior in the past

4- Take notes on each situation

5- Take the most important issue to focus on in the meeting

What will be the benefits?

You will have a better meeting this time and every time in the future once you start doing the same.

The key benefit will be that you will discover what you are good at.

You will talk about what is to be improved specifically, and not generic things.

Remember- all generic questions have generic answers.

You will form a specific strategy, the team will feel more confident to do better next time, and you will gain improved leadership skills. And you will build a strong and performing team.

Remember- You can give only what you have. So have good values.

# CONTINUOUS LEARNING

*Continuous learning is the basic requirement for success in any field- Brian Tracy.*

**WHY CONTINUOUS LEARNING?**

"Personal growth requires a mindset of continuous learning. This involves constantly seeking new knowledge, acquiring new skills, and remaining open to life's lessons. Being able to adapt and evolve is a defining trait of those who are committed to progress and self-improvement. The benefit of acquiring knowledge is that no one can take it away from you. You can share it with others to improve their lives. Continuous learning is the ongoing, voluntary, and self-motivated pursuit of knowledge and personal development. You need to examine and introspect your thoughts and actions. This will help you identify your strengths and where you need to improve. Self–reflection is the vehicle that will take you to the path of success.

I had a friend who was working with a pharmaceutical company and needed to earn better incentives, and the increments were lower than his expectations. He was depressed and was not concentrating on his job, and hence, improvement was not there. I met him after a few years, and he was very happy and shared his successful journey with me. I was very happy for my friend. I asked him what had helped you to reach this level. he shared it with me that day, and I gave credit to my new leader, who joined there after my previous boss transferred to some other place. Did you notice something here? Yes, he used "Boss" for his 1st Manager and "Leader" for his new Manager. I was interested in learning about the approach of his new manager, so I invited him to my place for dinner the next day, and I had the following learnings.

1- His second manager worked with him in the field and met many of his customers to observe his behavior, his approach to his customers, his communication, his product knowledge, and other skills.

2- He acknowledged his strong areas, like his communication and customer connection. and

3- Pointed out a few areas of improvement. He said I agreed with my manager that I needed to improve my product knowledge and data analytical skills.

4- Since there was open communication and his new manager was genuinely interested in his development, my friend accepted his suggestions and started working on those suggestions; he worked very hard and got the full support of his manager.

5- He acquired knowledge and refined his new skills.

The best part I noticed in him was that instead of viewing setbacks as failures, he took them as an opportunity to learn and improve.

This mindset shift enabled him to bounce back stronger. Over time, his approach of self-reflection and continuous learning has helped him, and his sales performance has always exceeded the sales targets. The reputation he built within the industry not only helped him to achieve financial success but also opened the door to leadership opportunities within the organization. Today, he is very successful in his role as Senior Business Leader.

This is the power of self-reflection and continuous learning!

Why should you learn continuously?

**STORY #1**

You might have heard this story many times, and many versions are available now. Originally, the story was written in 1940 with the title "Caps for Sale." I am sharing a new version to prove the point of continuous learning.

There was a cap seller in a village who was a hard-working person and was earning his bread by selling caps from village to village. It was a hot day in the summer season, and he was going from one village to another village; he was a little tired and thirsty too. He saw a garden and a water tap, so he went there, and after drinking the water, he lay down and fell asleep. In the garden, there were many naughty monkeys. They came down and took all his caps from the basket. When the cap seller got up, he saw the monkeys were these caps like him and were imitating him. He realized the fact that the monkeys were following his actions, so he took off the cap and threw it on the ground. Monkeys did the same, and he collected all his caps and went away happy.

After many years, the family business was transferred to the grandson of this cap seller. One particular day, The same thing happened to him that happened to his grandfather many years ago. He remembered the incident his grandfather shared with him, so immediately, he took off his cap and threw it on the ground.

He was hoping that monkeys would throw their caps, too, but to his biggest surprise, a baby monkey came down from a tree and took his cap, too. He wondered why these monkeys were not throwing their caps, and a baby monkey took his cap as well. In the meantime, this baby monkey came down and said to this cap seller—"Only you had a grandfather? I do have a grandfather who shared the same story with me".

Hope you have learned the lesson and are clear about the importance of continuous learning

Life is changing very fast, and so are requirements in the workplace. It is the need of the hour to keep yourself updated.

Why acquire new knowledge?

Why to learn new skills?

Many times, we come across people asking for someone's years of experience. It's a fair question, and the answer could range from a few months to many years. However, it's important to consider whether the experience has been one year of learning repeated over and over or if the person has had diverse learning experiences. To our surprise, some people may have been repeating the same learning over and over again but still need to improve their skills.

**EXERCISE FOR YOU**

List out the learnings that you had in the last one year

1.

2.

3.

Which skill you are using to do better than yesterday?

Which knowledge do you want to gain in the next 30 days?

# EMBRACE THE CHANGE

*The secret of change is to focus all of your energy on not fighting old but on building new Socrates.*

**WHY TO CHANGE?**

Change helps you to come out of your comfort zone. Change will make you learn new things and explore new opportunities. Never be resistant to change; it may prove very costly. Change should be slow, and as a leader, you should always be in a timely manner for change or to change. The advantage of being slow is you will avoid the problem of relapse (going back to old habits/practices, etc.). If you are making slow changes, then the chances of resistance from the team are less. It would be best if you were self-disciplined, and your approach should address the underlying cause of the problem while bringing about the change.

**STORY #1**

During my time as a Representative in a small city, I had a landowner who worked for a bank. At that time, computerization was starting to become prevalent, and bank employees were planning to go on strike against it. One day, while having tea with my landowner and a few other employees, I asked them what their concerns were. Their response surprised me, "They believed that they would all lose their jobs and that machines would take over everything they were doing.

I then asked them to imagine a scenario where all other banks had computers in their branches, but they were the only ones without one. Who would come to their branch? Would they be able to survive without a computer? This made them pause and discuss their next move.

The outcome of brainstorming and exchange of meaningful points was to prepare well and go for training to serve their customers better. Nowadays, it's easier to imagine a branch with a computer. You may have visited your branch only a few months or even years ago for banking purposes, but in the past, there used to be long queues for everything.

Instead of resisting change, they decided to embrace it. They attended various workshops and training sessions organized by their company. I am happy to share that last year, he finally retired from his position as a branch manager.

# SUMMARY

Let us revisit our learning.

Personal development is not just a choice but a continuous journey for great leadership.

As a leader, you have two Responsibilities

A- Team Building- Guiding team towards greater success

B- Self Development- because you can give only what you have.

These two responsibilities will make you an effective leader, and also you will contribute significantly to the overall success of your team.

**THE ESSENCE OF TEAMWORK: 1+1+1+1 IS GREATER THAN 4**

The essence of teamwork is the tale of collaboration, synergy, and shared achievement. Teamwork is the foundation on which great accomplishments are built. It is vital to understand what teamwork means. A team is a group of people with diverse perspectives, skills, and experience. When people with different cultures, backgrounds, and so on work together to tackle challenges from multiple angles, generate creative solutions, and achieve goals in time, it is teamwork.

The magic of teamwork lies in its ability to create synergy. This means that 1+1+1+1 is greater than 4. Team members feel accountable, promote strong work ethics, and improve efficiency and effectiveness. Good teamwork means that each team member understands their role and the impact it has on the overall objective. They work on their strengths and cover up the shortcomings of their team members, leaning on each other for encouragement and motivation.

With a team, you can achieve what you want to achieve. Therefore, it is important to develop a good team and foster a culture of teamwork. *"None of us is as smart as all of us"*- Ken Blanchard.

Communication is the backbone of collaboration. Clear and transparent communication ensures that all team members are on the same page regarding goals, tasks, and expectations. Create an environment where ideas can be freely exchanged, and people can share their feedback. It would be best if you created a foundation for mutual understanding.

Building trust is a key and very important aspect of teamwork. Cultivate an environment where team members feel secure in sharing their ideas and perspectives. The biggest advantage of trust will be an exploration of innovative solutions without fear of judgment.

### OVERCOMING CHALLENGES IN TEAMWORK?

You must be experiencing in your professional life that you are achieving collective success, but not without its challenges. A few of the challenges faced by leaders are – interpersonal dynamics, communication breakdown and differences in perspectives, and mismatch between individual goals and priorities with the team's objective. Lack of accountability.

During my initial days as a young leader, One day, my coach shared his ideas when I asked him a question on how to overcome these challenges, and his response gave me clarity and confidence. In his words

Teamwork is full of challenges, but every challenge brings opportunities for learning and growth. I always spend more time with my team to understand their aspirations, their priorities, and their strengths. I always give my team members opportunities to speak openly and appreciate them. I take responsibility for shortcomings but give full credit to them for the team's success. This helps me to cultivate trust.

When I asked him something more that made you an effective leader, the team became more successful. He explained the following with the help of the following diagram.

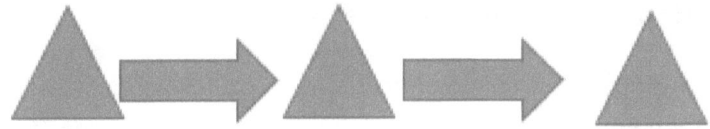

His first question was- what do I see here? I said, triangle. Only Triangle? I said three figures of triangle and arrow signs have connections among themselves. Good was his response, and then his explanation was as follows with a strong message for me to follow in my daily life as a professional.

He said the baseline is about foundation, and a strong foundation will make a good team and will help you foster teamwork. If you want a successful team, then you must spend time explaining the what very carefully.

What do you want?

What is a Task?

What is expected from each one of them? And must check for their understanding and, if need be, give more clarity.

What is the Objective of the team?

The next line in the triangle is about why. Why is it more important to explain the purpose behind that objective? "Otherwise, activity without purpose is meaningless."

Remember- Action is more than activity; it is Activity + purpose

I was more curious to know about 3rd line, but my coach was insisting on understanding these two aspects a little deep.

He asked a simple question to me.

Suppose your parents ask you to go to the market. What will be your first reaction or response? A reaction or response is your action, Right? Yes, that was my response.

Then I said, I am clear about What- Means Objective. I have to go to the market. His second question was if you go to the market without knowing the purpose, then, in excitement, I said- waste of time. He said good, but only time, I understood that I need to be a good listener, too. He continued, This happens to our team, and you may face such situations in life when you see people taking action without knowing their purpose or the purpose of the activity.

I said that in that case, I would ask my father or mother who is asking me to go to the market. Why should I go? He said, technically, you are right, but emotionally, it may sound like arrogant behavior. So, how do you ask about the purpose? It is art, but it is the responsibility of your parents to explain the task. As a team leader, you are in that role. I understood the message, and then he said about the 3rd line. The third line is about How it means your skills.

So it is – What- Why-How.

What is Objective

Why is the Purpose of that Objective and

How is Process? Now, see the image.

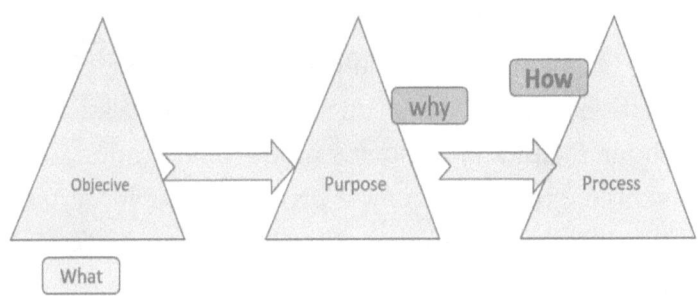

Your team members may be highly talented, but they need to know the purpose to save their talent in carrying out any activity.

He said, "In my professional life, I have seen many senior managers explain too much about the 'how' part. Actually, it is not required to explain 'how' so much. As a leader, you must spend time explaining 'what' and even more time explaining 'why' and less time explaining 'how.' Your team members already know how to do it; that's why they were selected for the organization. So, why should you explain 'how'? Only if someone is new to the role and needs to learn new skills; in that case, you must explain 'how' as well. Otherwise, work on the strengths of your team members and let them perform. I received a clear direction and a strong message for my leadership journey. I remain thankful to my mentor for the rest of my life for making me a good human being first, then making me a performing manager and good leader."

"The next session was about my doubts and provided a very clear way forward. Are you curious to know more? I appreciate your efforts and your decision to take action after knowing the purpose". My question was about **Leadership in Unity**. I want to know what I should do as a leader. His simple explanation was that it is a concept of effective leadership with clear boundaries and a framework of collaboration, cohesion, and shared purpose among a group of people or team. He explained to me the difference between a group of people and a real team. He said- group and team both have common features, individuals coming together; the difference lies in the level of interdependence, shared goals, clearly defined goals, and collaborative efforts. A team is characterized by a collective commitment to a common purpose, while a group may consist of individuals with more independent roles and less defined shared objectives.

On Leadership in Unity, he continued to help me to understand better. Tomorrow, you are going to play a very important role in fostering unity and harnessing the collective strength of the team towards goals. So, it becomes more important to understand the key aspects of leadership in unity. I requested him to share more about these aspects. I am happy to share the learnings that I got from my coach on leadership in unity.

Your key role will be to have a shared vision so that every team member is aligned toward a collective purpose.

Invite them to give their suggestions so they develop trust in you and start feeling that their opinion and ideas are valued by their leader.

Always make things simple; how can I do that? Was my question, and his response was simply by effective communication. What does effective communication mean in such a situation? His response made it so clear to me. If your team members feel comfortable in expressing their thoughts and concerns and information flows freely in the environment, it means you have made it.

What can keep my team united? It is so crucial to keep team members together in all situations. He, with a smile on his face, said- "Trust." Trust is foundational in the united team. You have to work very hard to build trust. If you can create trust, then they will take calculated risks and support each other, and you will achieve a common objective. I asked my coach if there was something more I should do. He said- there is no end, and you can keep thinking and keep learning still- I can suggest you empower your team members and support them, provide necessary resources, and guide them. I have experienced in my professional career that when people feel empowered, they try to give their best, and results are beyond your expectations. Still, I had a few doubts in my mind, and I, with his permission, asked a question: If there is conflict in the team, then what should I do?

First, he appreciated my question and said, yes, conflict may arise, but it will be your responsibility to address conflict promptly and, more importantly, constructively. This will help you to keep your team focused on its shared objectives. And he added further by suggesting to me.

Take advantage of every opportunity to celebrate success, and we must be together. Together means, was my question. And I got clarity when he said," A leader fosters a culture of celebrating collective achievements. You must acknowledge and appreciate the contributions of each team member; this will work like magic to motivate individuals to continue to work hard towards shared goals.

I learned very powerful lessons and tried to share my experience so you can save time. I suggest you guide your team through challenges. Be flexible, adjust to the situation, and make changes in your strategy if needed. Create an environment where individuals come together, utilizing their strengths, accepting each other as they are, and working to make the team a star team.

In the journey of building a high-performing team, remember that each individual will contribute, so accept them as they are, foster open communication, and cultivate a culture of trust.

Remember- "The collective strength of its members will define your team's success!"

Let me share one more thing that I learned from an Rtd Major from the Indian Army during a workshop for senior leadership. It was about-

**SYNERGY OF STRENGTHS**

During a workshop, we were tasked with building a boat using available resources and crossing a river while ensuring the safety of all team members. The objective was to use resources optimally while prioritizing safety. However, we needed help to achieve this as we either used resources excessively or compromised on safety. We were struggling with either overusing the resources or sacrificing safety.

It was at this critical juncture that a Major, a distinguished member of our team stepped forward as a guiding force. With a keen understanding of leadership, he directed our attention to a fundamental question: who among us was the designated team leader? Upon identifying the leader, the Major prompted the leader to identify the strengths, expertise, and weaknesses of each team member. He emphasized the importance of focusing on each team member's strengths and aligning them to complement one another.

He suggested that we focus on collaborative problem-solving, where we could combine diverse strengths to innovate and generate better solutions. He explained that this approach would maximize efficiency and optimize resources, and we should assign tasks to each team member based on their expertise.

In the end, it was this strategic intervention of the Major that not only guided us  across the rives safely abut also transformed us in to winning team. After we won the competition, we celebrated our success and noticed that we had a positive team culture because we leveraged each other's strengths. Ultimately, we learned that achieving collective goals should become a habit.

# LESSONS IN LEADERSHIP

## OWNING FAILURE, SHARING SUCCESS

A true leader always gives credit for success to his team and is always there to take responsibility for the team's failure. I am sharing a story by Shri A.P.J. Abdul Kalam (The missile man), Ex-President of India, in his own words...

Let me tell you about my experience. In 1973, I became the project director of India's satellite launch vehicle program, commonly called the SLV-3. Our goal was to put India 's 'Rohini' satellite into orbit by 1980. I was given funds and human resources — but was told clearly that by 1980, we had to launch the satellite into space. Thousands of people worked together in scientific and technical teams towards that goal.

By 1979 — I think the month was August — we thought we were ready. As the project director, I went to the control center for the launch. Four minutes before the satellite launch, the computer began to go through the checklist of items that needed to be checked. One minute later, the computer program put the launch on hold; the display showed that some control components were not in order. My experts — I had four or five of them with me — told me not to worry; they had done their calculations, and there was enough reserve fuel. So, I bypassed the computer, switched to manual mode, and launched the rocket. In the first stage, everything worked fine. In the second stage, a problem developed. Instead of the satellite going into orbit, the whole rocket system plunged into the Bay of Bengal. It was a big failure.

That day, the chairman of the Indian Space Research Organization, Prof. Satish Dhawan, had called a press conference. The launch was at 7:00 am, and the press conference — where journalists from around the world were present — was at 7:45 am at ISRO's satellite launch range in Sriharikota [in Andhra Pradesh in southern India ]. Prof. Dhawan, the leader of the organization, conducted the press conference himself. He took responsibility for the failure — he said that the team had worked very hard but that it needed more technological support. He assured the media that in another year, the team would definitely succeed. Now, I was the project director, and it was my failure, but instead, he took responsibility for the failure as chairman of the organization. The next year, in July 1980, we tried again to launch the satellite — and this time, we succeeded. The whole nation was jubilant. Again, there was a press conference. Prof. Dhawan called me aside and told me, 'You conduct the press conference today.'

### LEARNING

**Ownership of Failure-** Prof.Dhawan's willingness to take responsibility for the failure of the satellite launch demonstrates true leadership. It is a must for a leader to foster trust and accountability within their teams.

**Humility in Leadership-** This story highlights the humility of a leader who had authority and could have assigned the blame, but he chose to take responsibility for failure. This behavior helps leaders to earn respect and loyalty from their team members.

**Leading by Example-** Prof. Dhawan's actions are a classic example of leadership by example. Any leader who leads by example will cause his team to adopt a similar attitude. And above all

I learned –

**The Value of Experience over Theory.** Such experience, as shared by Sh A.P.J Abdul Kalam, can come from real-life experience, not by reading a book. So, always lead by example.

### A LESSON IN HUMILITY

In the early '90s, I owned a small chemist shop in a corner of the city. One morning around 9 AM, a disheveled man with an unshaven face walked into my store. Despite his worn appearance, he smiled warmly and complimented my Hero Honda Splendor motorcycle. Though I thanked him, I couldn't help but feel a bit skeptical, as such encounters often led to requests for money. However, to my surprise, he picked up a piece of cloth from my motorcycle and began cleaning the glass of it without saying anything.

After some time had passed without any communication between us, I decided to break the silence and asked him, "Do you need any help? Can I assist you in some way?" With a genuine smile, he replied with a powerful statement that would stay with me forever: **"Do you know someone who does not?"**

Stunned into silence, I could only watch as he finished cleaning my motorcycle. Inspired by his humility, I offered him tea and some hot snacks, providing him with a bit of money for his next meal. As he left, he bestowed his blessings upon me, leaving me with a profound lesson that transcended the moment.

This experience taught me a crucial lesson: no matter how successful one becomes or the heights achieved in one's career and personal life, everyone needs help. True generosity lies in giving what others may lack, whether it's a simple thank you, a smile, a genuine offer of assistance, or a compliment. In a world filled with individuals in need of necessities like food, shelter, and education, we all have the power to make a big difference. Let us do that!!

Let me take a break here, and I leave you with a wonderful story as shared by **Dr. Rajdeep Manwani, who happened to be Rahul Dravid's( Indian Cricket Team Coach and former captain) classmate while addressing a Sports Day Function:**

"During school, Rahul Dravid never attended classes regularly. He was always seen practicing in the nets. One day, he came to class and started writing notes with his gloves on. We were feeling uncomfortable seeing him writing with the gloves. Everyone was laughing, talking, whispering, but Rahul Dravid continued writing for that full hour.

After one hour was over, Rahul and I had a common friend, Adarsh, to whom Rahul asked, "Adarsh, can I borrow your account notes because exams are approaching and I haven't written many notes? I will Xerox it and give it to you back," Adarsh replied. "Rahul, I'll give you those notes, but you have to tell me why you are wearing gloves all the time. You came to class wearing gloves, and you continued wearing them; you were wearing them even when the teacher was dictating notes. Is it to impress Anupama? (Anupama was the most beautiful girl in their class!). Rahul Dravid said, "No...no, she is already impressed; I don't have to impress her."

"Then why did you wear the gloves all the time?" I asked. Rahul Dravid shared with me something that was a very interesting day.

He replied, "You know something, Adarsh? In the last two Ranji matches that I played, I wore my old gloves, which were very loose. Because it was loose, whenever the bowler bowled and the ball went past my gloves, it created a snicking sound. The wicketkeeper caught it, he appealed, and both times, even though I didn't touch the ball, I was caught behind. I thought to myself,' No, this can't continue,' and so I bought these gloves, and I want to get accustomed to wearing these new gloves. I want my hands to sweat into these new gloves. So, for the next 48 hours, I will wear these gloves continuously because the next Ranji match, which is a semi-final, is just two days away. I want my hands to sweat in and get adjusted to the gloves. I am not going to remove the gloves even when I am sleeping, even when I am eating, even when I am coming to class because I want to do well in the next match, and I want my hands to be comfortable in those gloves".

The very next match was their semi-finals against Saurashtra, and he scored a century. In the finals, Karnataka played against Delhi that year, and he scored another century. Based on those two performances, he was selected for the Indian cricket team, which went to England. Surprisingly, in the first test match in England, he scored 90 odd runs (England vs. India, 2nd Test ) when Sourav Ganguly scored a century, and the rest, as they say, is history.

Rahul was willing to wear those gloves for 48 hours, even when it was uncomfortable, or it was hot. He was sweating in those gloves for 48 hours continuously because he wanted to excel in what he was doing. He took responsibility for himself for his performance. Rahul never complained a single time, nor did he argue against any Umpire's decision. He never said even once that the wicketkeeper was unethical. He knew that he didn't touch the ball, and even then, they appealed to get him out. He took responsibility for his own life. He had a very strong internal locus of control.

With this, I invite you to embark on a transformative exploration of growth and personal empowerment through the lens of various experiences and challenges.

This is episode no two under the umbrella of our Series" Rise to Thrive."

Before I close here, let me revisit our learnings. In episode 1, we saw how Ramdas helped us learn from the wisdom of his Guru Ji. We learned the core elements of exceptional leadership. Focused on the philosophy of identifying and mastering the singular element that can transform one's leadership capabilities. "The One Thing"- the 1st book in this series has key principles such as prioritization, goal setting, and strategic decision making, all geared towards honing effective leadership skills. The book " The One Thing"- has engaging anecdotes and real-world examples that can propel leaders toward leadership excellence.

In episode 2- " How to Go Beyond Strength," we have key themes such as goal setting, problem-solving, positive thinking, success, happiness, and the pivotal role of information in achieving success.

We can draw inspiration from the story shared by Dr. A.P.J Abdul Kalam, former President of India; "The real power of Inspiration." The narrative concludes with another story from a classmate of Rahul Dravid, the coach of the Indian Cricket team- offering an excellent example of resilience, determination, and the transformative impact of these principles on real-life success stories.

# MY BEST WISHES TO YOU

**I am confident that this book, "How to Go Beyond Strength," will serve as a roadmap for individuals like us who are seeking not just success but a fulfilling and purpose-driven life.**

So get ready to wear something you are uncomfortable with at this point.

If yes- what is that?

Make a  perfect plan and move on.

"Perfect Planning Prevents Poor Performance"

Thank you for reading my book, and I am sure you will start a journey to **Go Beyond Strength.**

*"Strength and Growth comes only through continuous efforts and struggle"- Napoleon Hill.*

# WITH

# GOOD WISHES

## FOR A

# BETTER

# TOMORROW!!!

# ABOUT THE AUTHOR

 JP Pathak emerges as a seasoned professional in the realms of sales, management, training, and coaching, with a remarkable journey spanning over 35 years. As a dedicated student of sales and management, he has honed his expertise not only as a practitioner but also as a mentor, guiding individuals to discover their **"One Thing"** that propels them toward realizing their dreams and purpose.

Throughout his extensive career, JP has navigated the intricacies of sales and marketing, earning a reputation as a sales superstar in his own right.

One of JP's distinctive qualities lies in his ability to simplify complex concepts, making them accessible and understandable for his audience. His training and coaching methods are infused with a touch of humor, creating an environment that fosters relaxation and comfort, even in challenging situations or when dealing with difficult-to-manage individuals.

JP's effectiveness as a trainer is not solely based on his vast experience but is also enriched by his capacity to weave anecdotes and small stories into his teachings. These narratives serve as memorable lessons, ensuring that the knowledge imparted remains ingrained in the minds of his students for an extended period.

By incorporating humor and storytelling, JP not only imparts wisdom but also creates an engaging and enjoyable learning experience.

Beyond his professional endeavors, JP Pathak is a science graduate who shares his life with his wife and two daughters. His commitment extends beyond individual growth, as he actively contributes to the development of both people and organizations. Through his training and coaching initiatives, JP leaves an indelible mark on the journey of those he guides, fostering growth and success.

# DISCLAIMER

This book is for informational purposes only. Readers acknowledge that the author does not render legal, financial, medical, or professional advice. The content within this book has been derived from various sources. Please consult a licensed professional before attempting any techniques outlined in this book.

By reading this document, the reader agrees that under no circumstances is the author responsible for any direct or indirect losses incurred as a result of the use of the information contained within this document, including but not limited to errors, omissions, or inaccuracies. Adherence to all applicable laws and regulations, including international, federal, state, and local governing professional licensing, business practices, advertising, and all other jurisdictions, is the sole responsibility of the purchaser or reader. Neither the author nor the publisher assumes any responsibility or liability whatsoever on behalf of the purchaser or reader of these materials. Any perceived slight of any individual or organization is purely unintentional.

# MAY I ASK YOU A FAVOR?

At the outset, I want to give you a big thanks for reading this book. You could have chosen any other book, but you took mine, and I appreciate this. I hope you have at least a few actionable insights that will positively impact your daily life.

Can I ask for 30 seconds more of your time?

I'd love it if you could leave a review of the book. That will help me grow my readership by encouraging folks to take a chance on my books.

**Keeping it straight -** *reviews are the lifeblood of any author.*

It will take less than a minute of your time but will tremendously help me reach out to more people. **Kindly provide your review at the store you bought this book from.** And I'd love to see your review. Thanks for your support.